The Willow's Silence

THE FAOINSGEUL WOODS

MOLLY LIKOVICH

MARCIA RUIZ-OLGUÍN

To the Cathars, may the fates allow our encounter.

"Why do you do this?"

"I like to do it. I enjoy it. Take your aesthete's: taste purer things; kill them swiftly if you will, but do it. For do not doubt: you are a killer."

— INTERVIEW WITH THE VAMPIRE

ALCHEMIA HALL

Let's start with the ending. A girl runs away.
She was made of tea leaves and broken
promises. Mulled wine and ancient prophecies.
French stories wrapped up in an English name.
And she came here to be in love.
Oh how we failed her.

Hold your breath when the carriage crosses
through the gate. We can never be too
sure. Maybe *their* ghosts are
here as well. Hiding between
all the heartache—all the reflections.
Love is lost here, or so they say.

This house is made up of girl-bodies.
The firmament shakes with the rattling
of their bones. The wallpaper peels
with the sound of their cries.
Some nights it feels like the house is melting.

                I remember it here.

It got so cold so quickly. But I am sun-soaked
now. The dawn-dappled moors are a part of me.

There was a staircase in the woods beyond
these moors beyond these wicked walls.
But I'm getting ahead of myself.
Let me take you back.

There was absolutely no possibility of taking

                a walk that day...

Oh wait, maybe those words aren't my own.
But they're all ours anymore, aren't they?

Are you listening?
Let's begin.

THE OATH OF ISABELLA

"We will return again in 700 years when the laurel turns green."
-The Cathar Prophecy

Prologue

The heat of the French summer, deep in the hills
of Mary Magdalene's believers. The Caravan
blew in on a willow's wind and swept my soul
up in thistle milk tea leaves and magic 8 balls
yet to be named as such.
It was so very long ago. They were what I had
been waiting for. An invitation to become the stuff of myth.
I left. Under a full moon,
colorful sleeves on my arms, sugar on my tongue.

The True Start of the Story

Over green, laurel-laden hills full of smiling men
and laughing women. Fires that danced before
my ill eyes, hearts that beat louder
than the stars. I met him. He danced
candle-flame close and scoffed at the 'heretics'
I dared share sacrament with. (Our holy rites
looked nothing like his—candle-lit confessionals,
ash and smoke; we were the blaze itself).
The Mary Magdalene hills faded away
in his eyes, the smoke blurred with the dust
when I left in his arms. My ancestors
always said they'd come again. Why didn't I wait?

*The Part Where We Begin to Doubt. There Aren't Enough Pages Left to
Resolve This Pain*

I crossed an ocean, left my beautiful France behind.
On English streets I wondered
if this is what it feels like to fade?
The wedding band, golden, promising—an ouroboros full
of songs I had forgotten how to sing.
Alchemia Hall, clad in looming iron gates and ghosts
thicker than the winter air. Words
can become fists as fast as love can become
hate and memories can become aches.
The snow drowned the vampiress on the lawn,
and muted the souls singing
from the rooftop. The dead girl in the oratory told me
to abandon prayer. Love
isn't supposed to bruise, passion is meant to bleed.
The wanderers had taught me that women
can press their hands together too.

Something Like an Epilogue

My Cathars had been right all along.
Being loved doesn't mean standing still.
The years will end by the time I find my heart, and build
a house, and love the way he could never love me.
500 years is not such a long time to wait. I am the
magic his holy men wish they had.

The laurel graves will turn green and the righteous
shall finally inherit the earth. Travelers
will seek me out. I will make a home in the darkness.
I will hold the light in my hands to show wanderers' the
way out

The Pages Have Run Out. But The Writer Has Given Us Hope.

This house will not hold me.
I will leave again, in two years,
when the willow's silence is deafening.

LEAVE THE GHOST

This house has been empty for so long. It used to hold
stories. I played
at being a lady better than any con artist
out on those noisy New Orleans
streets. I'm not like Isabella. I never used tea.
Now I sip smoky bits of the woods and pretend I can

still breathe. I kept my devils
even in death. I dazzled
the world once upon a pulse.

I let so many women slip
through my fingers. Honeyed-and lonely

I tried to forget these strange tea-apparitions, sinking
moons, and meaningless
prophecies written for girls who know
how to swim.

But there's no forgetting devil property
and belladonna. I became one of those
street performers with tarot card-heavy pockets.

I was so busy trying not to drown that I wasn't
looking at the boy in the sun begging me

                    to breathe. I'm not a horse to be made

to drink. My lungs will carry this fortune-teller tragedy
as long as I walk this realm. Being

loved doesn't mean staying still.

I'm at the harbor now. The ships are off their mooring.
Please don't say goodbye.

PRIMA

It begins the way it always does in black and white.
I've been here before. I know the ghosts by name.

This pain bleeds away into the swirling colors of that cursed
night. Apple-coated

teeth. A world where I was praised just for breathing.
I was warned:

> *play your hand very carefully, little
> girl.* I sold sleep and dreams for this.

This is just a dream. I used to be scared. But I've been
here before. I know these memories by name.

Paintings that hang on the walls of my mind
when the stars come out.

A blue taffeta dress, a dagger behind my back. Blade
cutting my palm red. My ribcage wrapped in ribbons.

He caged even my breathing.

He painted me in his mind; he paints me now, dancing with him—
our kiss stopping time.

If my sister ever asks for me, tell her she can find me trapped in his mind.
Stretched across

a chaise lounge, a glass of absinthe in my hand. My dress
(made of pearls or dying butterflies) strangling me as we dream

our most elaborate nightmare together.
If you ever miss me, write my name down in blood,
address it to the stars.

13

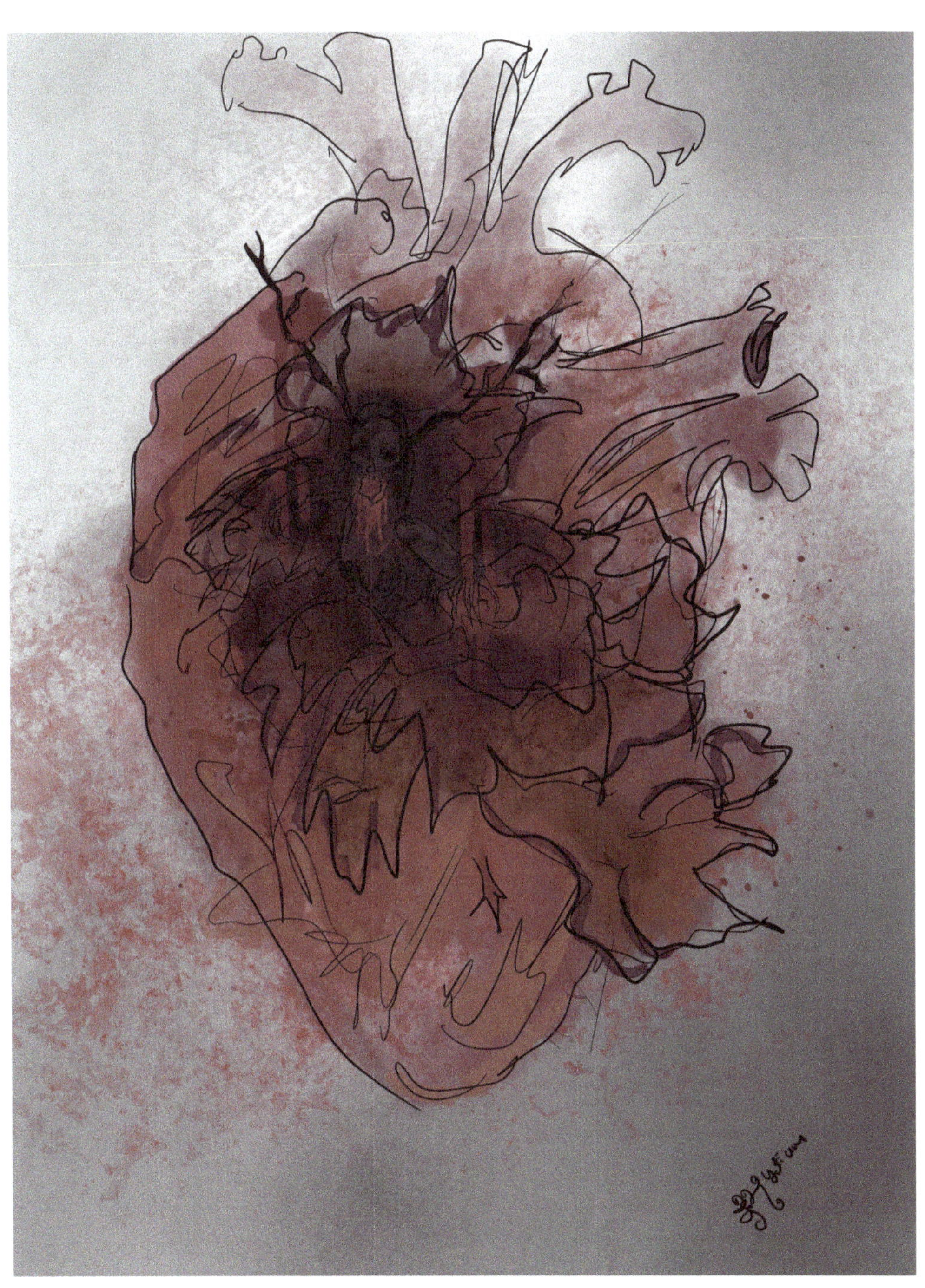

WORDS FROM THE MOUTH OF THE BEARER OF
VICTORY

we rattled on the floor like pearls. molars as loud as drums.
he can hear us. we've been so loud for so long. but the rain—
the rain overtook us. swallowed up our sounds along with her
screams. look how beautiful we are when we break.
do you think she loved us the way he loved her?
we suppose we'll never know now. the canines were knife-
sharp, but still her mouth was muffled by his.
was this a true fear of the great poet?
to hold such specific pain in his
palm? a place meant for eucharist.
how loud do the men in the stories
scream when they realize their
brides are just a collection of
cavities and grave dirt
here on the floor of a study
full of stories she won't get to tell.
the stone is too heavy now.

LJUBIM TE

I. Italian: from the medieval female personal name Bella, meaning 'beautiful', 'lovely'.

On dark and dreary nights draped in plum-
colored sheets and whispers from another

world is when she learned the power
of these misremembered legends.

The beach town looked different once
she knew what blood tasted like.

It makes perfect sense that this should
happen.

She could build empires inside her heart
from how relentlessly she loved. Her empathy

brought gods to their knees. There's nothing
more powerful than a teenage
girl.

II. from the Middle English personal name Edward, Old English Eadward, composed of the elements ead 'prosperity', 'fortune' + 'guard'.

Protector in the shadows, bathed in starlight.
He'd never think so highly

of himself. He is
better in her eyes. Burdens can grow

heavy after centuries of guilt.

He wanted nothing more than to live

in the empire she built inside
herself. To climb the marble pillars of

her cathedral and pledge his allegiance
to loving her.

Who cares if they mock this story?
It changed the world.

STEP RIGHT UP

we will have fun // a carnival of screams like symphonies // her hands full of suicides unacted on and i have waited too long // this is how someone learns to love a beast // an old movie in an older heart and her young eyes infect every dying thing // she is horribly alive and i will curse // anyone

MOTH-WINGED

-Crimson Peak

I thought I had gotten the hang of blaming and breaking hearts so I could
rebuild them with pen and ink; typewriter ribbons

and the blood of ghosts. I survived
the bones of a house made of winter. I survived you.

All crimes are perfect in their own way. When you make lungs
into ghosts, it is a success no matter the cost.

In the stories it takes me
sixteen nightgowns to win. High-collared, buttoned tight.

You flowed like midnight winds—full of witches
and broken promises.

They'll tell you this was all fiction. And to be quite plain,
I don't believe a word of it myself.

GARDEN OR ORCHARD

> *"You must come with me, loving me, to death."*
> -Carmilla by Joseph Sheridan Le Fanu

a bed made of blood from years of this. men
with nails. hammers
to judge. fists that turn to jury. fears that become executioner.
and yet, *you* make sense.

the folk songs they sing in the market burn me
worse than the water your father has blessed with beliefs.

can you forgive me for the sins i pray you never
know? learn to love me despite how much

rot lives inside my bones?

i will love you. ardently. like the stuff of storybooks
i'm sure your mother read to you. once. upon

dreams and nightmares and memories we once wove
together. fated to remain like this.

you know i was destined to know you? your white blonde
hair like virgin snow, not yet trodden by heavy, commanding

boots. your eyes that long to be loved. your lips
that beg to be kissed.

nobody knows us in this bed. my hands on you are more
beautiful than their altars. i would kneel before you

if you promise

to never seek to know who i am and what've i've been, back
before the horses ran me off your road.

GIVE ME PEACE

I said I won't leave you—to
her. Right choices can look wrong
in the most perfectly dimmed

candlelight. Rain-soaked, cliche
my red-hearted confidant. Lover
of light to your moth-dark flame.

She knows how to say *I love him* as well
as I do. I'm not lying when my red lips
imprint upon your skin. You ended her.

The wolves are yours. I can see
the knives in your mouth.
The drumming of my heartbeat is deafening.

I want the silence of your chest.
The ice of your kiss.

Take me
away. Death rots

in the shade of rubies on an ornate cross.
Let me learn from the most beautiful

beast. Let me love with the
fiercest condemnation.

I would sooner burn these
holy palaces to the ground before

I'd leave. Call the winds. Howl
with those wolves I once feared.

I have waited a thousand,
thousand lives to die with you.

You sailed a sinking ship across an ocean
of ticking clocks to find me

here. My bones are
too heavy with the dying the living must know.

End it.
I love you too much to let you save me.

DEAD BLOOD

I drink from empty communion cups. There is no
seat for me at god's table. But we don't all long
for ivory and pearl; we bathed in gold in my day.

I rearranged stars for him. Made constellations
out of his broken promises. I'm only

the villain in his soliloquies. If there were history books
these would just be wars I had won. Gallantly saving
the meek from Death (for oh, how it loves its prey).

    I loved him. Let that be known within these walls.
    Even if all that ever remains are the ghosts.

INTERESTING TIMES

The witches nodded when they saw me buy ginger, and ginseng,
and turmeric. The wise woman smiled and laughed as I gathered
berries by her house deep in the wood. I know I'm lost. But I must keep
going.

Then there was you. Bold and beautiful.
Like the brushstrokes of Degas made up in a person.

Marvelous. You asked me for answers. The witches
know why I couldn't
tell you.
My words will scratch and claw their way out of my throat
for as long as men like you look at women like me—
grab our wrists as we reach for anise. Question every cup
of chamomile tea we pour. If I can't ward away
your voice then let me protect my veins from your

hands. Teeth tugging and tongue licking
at the satin I keep around my words. A neck
like a skyline. A lie like a poem. Say you love me
long enough and loud enough that I can pretend
to believe
it. You still look so good in the morning before
I am awake enough to remember
that you are the villain in my romance. Your hands are my guillotine.

I never said I wanted to live through 'interesting
times.'
Just that I wanted
to live.

42

There are devils here in my heart
and I am not afraid.
Untie the ribbon, my love.
See who is full of fear once you see all of me.
And if anyone between the two of us is to be The Fool,
let it be me.
Drink my tea. Choke on my words.
And I will live
forever.

THE MEANING OF BLUE

the world is so dark outside. the wind is full
of wild things that bite.

that's what he told me. he made locks look
like such pretty things. and my god was i

a pretty thing. murder does not make
monsters of us all.

will you love him? as fiercely as you know how?
with bloodcloaked keyholes and knife-sharp

mirrors. the feel of his
hips snapping against yours—

a symphony of gore. bricks surrounding
a dozen eyes that once held the same

hope as you do now. but good god
he looks so miraculous when he smiles.

they don't teach this kind of love
in school. it is a secret grandmothers

keep hidden away in music boxes.
the sound of his breathing must be

your music now. the ghosts are
real, this much you know.

MAKE MONSTERS OF US ALL

They said a love this horrific should have faded away
with the death of our child-bodies. There shouldn't

still be blood in the bathtub. I shouldn't have to make
anymore tea. Maybe I maimed his heart. But this house

twisted mine. The sweat and sugar of these rooms
where we were never allowed to play.

The madness I wove into piano keys just so that
I didn't have to hear the heartbeat of this house.

I saved a souvenir of my success.
Buried it down here with the peak's blood and his

failures. The sound the snow makes against the swing
of the cleaver is the wedding bells he and I

will never hear. I am a vicious
thing, I know. But all this horror—

it was for love.

WHAT TO DO IF THE CANDLE SUDDENLY LIGHTS ITSELF

52

Don't whisper. The gods are listening. Or a lesser demon. Either way, breathe in the fire and thank it (most likely *her*) for the light. Tuck the hermit card into your dress and walk up the stairs, don't let the ghosts haunt you any longer. Walk among them. Hear their stories. Remember their names.

MO CRIDHE

I asked her to let our souls encounter like the rain meets the river. I plead
to her in poetry as we broke bread over other lovers' bones. Candle-lit

vigils for a soul spent across seven years. Under the gaze of the waning
moon and shimmering stars, we danced with cloth-bound hands

and love-heavy hearts. We were sweet summer children and I *was*
in love. I sat in Arthur's chair and saw her face. Cut open my chest,

scooped out my truest self and laid it bare before you; watched as you
took me in your hands. *Do you see her?* I asked.

Now I wonder if you ever even saw me. I still sing our song in the
shower,
if I listen closely I can hear the universe singing along. Threads woven so

tightly I wonder if the stars will ever undo them. I was your strength and
you were
my weakness. Is she even listening? When did you become

such a ghost? Maybe I just burned too bright to be loved by a soul
so dim. Stay in the darkness. I make these vows to the fire now.

NIGHTSHADE

My cheeks glowed peach-pink
back when I was something
you could love. A midnight

mistress full of promises
of something better.

I *am* better. I am more.
(more than her)

This magic comes in pieces.
Blows in on the wind, beats me down
with the rain. Maybe she

folded herself into your bruising
embrace better than me. I tried to

bloom into the night the way
wisteria blooms across every inch
of skin that's been caressed

by your cruelty. But it was
so beautiful to burn. You made
craters here and I melted

my skin trying to carve
them away.

The moon howls for me—
scratches at my back, begging me
to turn around. Why am I running
so fast? Why am I chasing

ghosts?

The moon is all I have now.
Candle wax on waning skin.
I don't know when (if ever)
I'll be full again.

But I was better.
I was more than any pretty,
rosy-cheeked innocent could ever be.

MY HOLOFERNES

here in this bed, i first showed you
my bones and you scratched my hips raw.
the winter is yelling at
the door. snowfall-jagged claws tearing at
us. come closer and remember
how to hold me. i remember
how to

                    throw the blade at the wall—

you sound so sad when
you scream.

this wounded Animal bleeds
like snow. shipwrecked dresses
around a touch-starved creature.
a melted
winter storm. hollow
like our hearts.

the door splinters beneath
our feet. is this violence you
or the wind? why do you

look so scared with your blood
between my thighs?

how loud will you 'love'
me? how hard will i beg?
i sharpen my knife over ocean-wet
rocks. i love the way your heart
looks when your collar-
bones aren't blocking the view.

the way this winter fits inside your body
when there aren't 24 bones
in the way.

light your candles. applaud your
god. all i hear is the wolves at the door.

BLESSINGS OF THE DEEP THAT LIES BELOW

Come in, Wanderer. Brush the thistle and brambles
from your coat—light
a candle and let me tell you a tale.

          King Asa said it was quite alright for men to make their
                    fiction

fact. Smashed the pithois, washed away the murals.
Boarded her
up, hid her away. Made her memories myth.

Consort of the supreme god. Sacred whore. Baal's lover, a christian liar.
So many names for just me. Water and words. Blood and wine.
Sacrifice me on mountaintops if you must but save the statues for all
the daughters. Sea salt sweet on my tongue.

Foolish boys playing god.
You cannot drown a sea queen.

Remember me in the whispers. *Cult objects* passed between broken
bones, hands tired of applauding a dead man in an empty sky.

You can blow out the candle now, dear Wanderer. Traveler. Forest-
bound
lover. I don't know how you got here, but wherever you go next—

remember Asherah. However you wish to tell them I *was* when I
drew sacred breath. Before this house became a hollow home.
Before girl-ghosts made up the firmament we stand beneath.

Before.
Before.
Before.

I was once before. Now I'm only memories.
Myth.
Fiction.
Fact.

HIGHER GROUND

I finally found hell and it's so peaceful here. The creature you tied
down, kept back—with needle and thread—is an old friend. I welcomed
it with open arms.

Is my body haunted, you ask. If I tell you, you might not go in.

You begged for me to haunt you. I am made up of the same stuff as you.

My soul and yours—twin fires made of frost and flame.

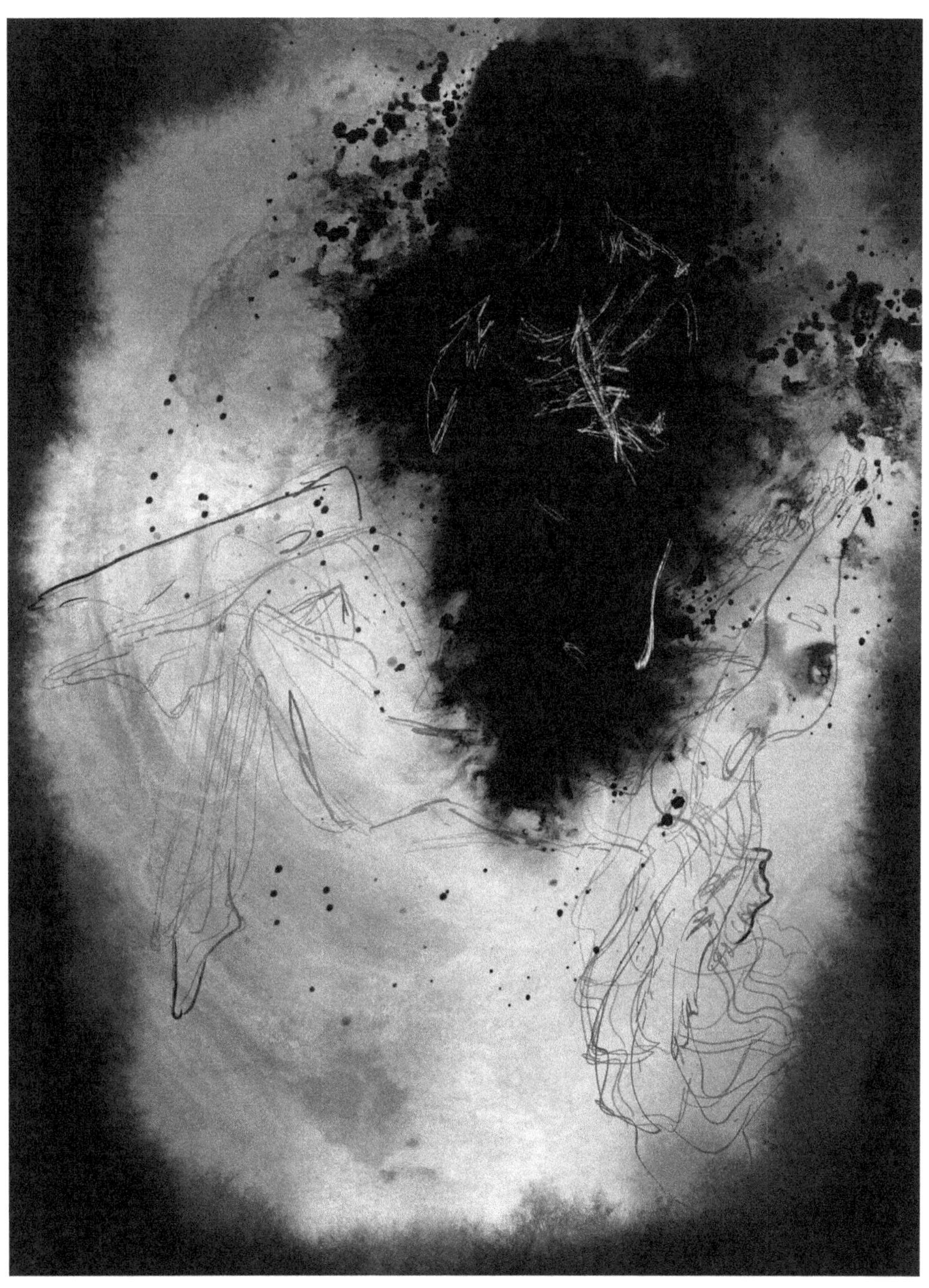

LOTUS

You must think that every story inside this house's bones is one of sorrow. Mirrors make a mess of everything, they show lies where there are merely folktales. Roses mean something different here. Would you drink his wine? Read his Shakespeare and call him lover? Could you love like she did? Gods know every ghost girl here wishes to have had what she did beneath those forbidden sheets. Primal and wanton. Gothic and drowning. We can still hear the phantoms of their long lost passions within these haunted halls.

THE MOORS PROPHECY

This is where I went breathless into a night I never wanted
to end. Ending meant facing
the empty space. Laces that must be untied by my own hands.
Wearing white only for mourning. Like lillies in
a winter-soaked pond.
Will dying out here hurt any less than at a loveless table
with real love's pretty lies whispering on the wind?

I think I must. Save

judgment for the pretty paperback romance
novels all the girls who shunned me back in school
loved to hide beneath their frocks. I'd
rather dine with an unhandsome heart.

The sound is ethereal. I'm scared.
But I've been here before.

ASTERIA

Bet-el-geuse (n)/Betelgeuse is usually the tenth-brightest star in the night sky and, after Rigel, the second-brightest in the constellation of Orion.

How do all these stories start?

"Once upon a time?"

Yes? Alright then

THE EMPRESS

Once upon a time there was a
creation
of life in the heart of a dying girl
in a house full of
the dead. Can you see
her now? Rooftop beneath
boots and songs unsung in her
eyes. Hollywood
tricked you into
thinking he was
the teller of this tale. But when
two are in love,
the story
belongs
to both.

KNIGHT OF CUPS

He habitually charms. Every
woman a snake
ensnared in his basket.
Like any good story, she is the
exception
She looks so lovely when she loves
him. He holds nothing but
immortality. Lifetimes lived in
death. Invisible
in every way—
and her cup overfloweth so long ago
that not even the gods
can remember.
The games she played were
dark ones.
Better spirits warned her—
and his hands made her forget

TWO OF CUPS

Their love was the kind that could end
bloodlines.
Rage wars. Both sides guilty.
They make
beautiful ghosts and horrid lovers and
they are absolutely,
terribly
suited for each other.

THREE OF SWORDS

Violent delights. Violent ends.

THE HERMIT

Are you like me? Begging
her to go back down that stair-
Case. Into his arms.
Fold herself inside
the pages of the almanack
in his hands.
The only place that makes any
sense.

What is it the witches say?

"By the power of three times three?"

THE LOVERS

She whispers against the rain,
with a heart made of moors

love me till i'm me again.
And he does.

Yes?

Alright then.

III

THE *VÉRITÉ* REFLECTION

I did not have it in myself. The bronze
age of elephants and jumping spiders. The waves
of sounds that kept me up at night in a half-empty
bed. You reach for me but you never reach

me. It's over now.
This music has deafened you.
Fifteen feet high rocks stand on this soil you stole
me away to.

I used to be a visage
forged from flames. Scalding tea.
Cups full of fortunes. Don't you wish
you were me?

I know how to endure.
Rusted red welts in the shape
of you. I will never sleep in another bed
that holds the shape of you.

The pool of knowing myself shows
me *myself*
back when I was a part of
the Cathar prophecy. Back when I was made

of moon-kissed skin, stars, and hope.
Now I am made of shattered bone china,
creaking floorboards, and endings.

I will always

regret you.

This is the ugly history

of beautiful things.

RIONNAG

unspool me. the stories said we were
sturdier than this. but you can't trust the tongues of
unwanted things. even faeries have

to give up at some point.
but don't we look so beautiful when we end?
don't i look so pretty behind the doors

you forgot how to knock on?
i wove my end myself this time.
refused to let your river water-soaked words

downfall me. maybe i can be the warning.
let the other women find me before they
become ghosts themselves.

we can't change endings that have already
ended. i can't be an ocean for you.
and you never could believe me.

but i knew everything once.
i know everything now.

THIS IS NOT THE BOOK OF LOVE

This is where the story is
meant to end. In a biblical burning. Where I lay
down with my ancestors and wait for centuries.
Maybe I will come back, until then you will hear
my voice on the wind. Every time you brew
a cup of tea you'll see my face in the leaves.

       I shouldn't have to be the one to burn when his bones

are so wicked. They break so beautifully. His purpling, reddening skin
looks like all those paintings of my homeland
that he wouldn't let me hang.

They've spent so many years killing witches. When they grew
tired of how our flesh smelled when we burned, they chose
ropes and rocks.

       I came this far. Crossed an ocean to learn to have

the upper hand. I think he calls such a thing *love.*

The people in town have called our house *Alchemy Hall*
for his magnificent feat of turning
the ghoulish girl from Gaul
into gold.

       I can't make gold, but I am more.

mettle than he bargained for. I can't spin
straw into gold but I can brew thistle and milk
into tea. He never should have let me tend
my garden if he wanted
to keep the witch out of *me.*

But don't worry.

       I won't turn his home to ruins the way

his ancestral conquerors destroyed the chateau.

Maybe that's where I'll go. Maybe those ghosts still
haunt the hills where the holy hall once stood.

I'll walk through those hills and feel
the grass beneath my feet again.

MY SOUL DEMANDS YOU

Home used to smell of cinnamon and honeysuckle. Now it reeks of
ghosts.
Everlasting gloom—like paint—chips at the edges. But I'll
always wish for specters—gleams and glints of you.
These bones will never be weary of the burden of you. Your
haunting is not something I long to escape.
Carve me up like Autumn gordes and paint me in memories. I'll
always be
lost in these halls—on these hills–
if I'm always waiting for you.
Forever you promised to haunt me, yet you haven't given me even
one day.
Forever, you said. *Forever.*

IRONLESS

Honey-soaked heart. There's so many bees
in here. Their buzz rattles the glass. Can I pretend
I don't see them? Not the bees.

   The faces like clay. Maybe I should be
   startled. Maybe I should ache.

I do. Gods, I do.
The Cathars never spoke of this.

I don't know how I can break anymore.
Her story is so heavy on my skin.
Their stories are so loud in my head.

   I think the mirror can hear my
   breathing.

I tie ribbons around my
wrists and promise I won't
forget them.

   Promise me you won't forget.

   Memorize the bones
   of this story.
   Memorize me.

I won't let the wind rattle
this glass. I won't let the ghosts
rattle me.

When you make it to the moors, say a prayer
for the suicidal girls in the dying house.

THE UNMADE SEASON

The Darkest Timeline

Mina Harker in life. Jane Eyre in death.
A candle without
a wick. Lungs full of river
water. Indentations in the shape
of 'god's' hands.

I chose a name of danger and betrayal.
Berry-stained words on my silver
stage. Steamboat railing beneath my

hands and Jenny's voice mixing with Jack's off
the rushing water.

It's no surprise. The stars were the only
ones in attendance at my funeral.

[Everything that came after made me nothing more

than the footnote in someone else's story. I am a

leading lady through and through, never forget that.]

The French Timeline

Traveling fortune tellers came to the city
and dazzled. I would see her
face again. In a decade. She was a wife
then and I was the poor, uneducated witchling
playing at hedonism onstage.

By the time I found Alchemia Hall she was long

gone. Lost to the moors and deep
in the Faoinsgeul Woods.

I could go there too.
I could be someone too.

The Third Timeline

There is a cottage deep in the woods.
Past the rabbit hole, through the Goblin Grove (bow
to the King as you pass through), across the honeyed-sea
and up the staircase they tell you not to climb.

Within the walls sits a witch divining over tea-leaves
and the ghost of a great sorceress learning how to make
it rain.

DOMICILE

"The dry yellow heath of the moors rose around us on all sides. It was like walking on the sun."
-Amy Wolf

Wise women walked these hills. You can hear
it in the wind. Wingless things always fight
to keep birds, but we rattle those cages until they break.
I used to be made of glass and tea leaves. Now it's all
thistle and thorns; milk-honey words gone away
with the winters I'll choose not to remember.

Their ghosts call to me out here. Voices like birdsong.
Because hope has wings and girls have souls
and have you ever seen anything as beautiful
as dawn on the moors.

"Curses only have power when you believe in them. And I don't."

-Practical Magic

Acknowledgments

To those ancient specters that wander the proverbial moors of our hearts and minds and souls, we thank thee for guiding us through the darkness.

To Emily and Charlotte Brontë we thank you remarkable ladies for creating Jane and Cathy, they fueled the creation of this absurdly gothic narrative.

To Guillermo Del Toro we are eternally grateful that you had a practical set built for *Crimson Peak* so that while crafting this strange story we were able to watch Jessica Chastain run around madly with a meat cleaver. It inspired us endlessly.

To the raven that tormented Edgar Allan Poe, thank you for your service.

Thank you to Lestat for being so insane. We needed it.

To our friends and family who believed in this journey deeper into the Faoinsgeul Woods.

And lastly we thank the Cathars. You are not forgotten.

About the Authors

MOLLY LIKOVICH

Molly is a poet, a romance author, weaver of spells, and chanter of incantations. A gothic leading lady in her own right, her novella *Riding The Headless Horseman* was a #1 Amazon Bestseller and her short poems and stories have appeared in *Shore Poetry, Fahmidan Review,* and *Love Letters to Poe Vol. 3* among many others. She currently lives in the distant, mythical land of the Eastern Shore of Maryland with her two familiars and many, many books. Learn more about her at molly-likovich.com

MARCIA RUIZ-OLGUÍN

In between a haunted corner and a whimsical door, Marcia Ruiz-Olguín spends her time away conjuring things out of metal, ink, and paper. With a wireless stylus as her wand and strangeness and charm as her ingredients. She has a BA in Literature from La Universidad de las Américas Puebla and a Certificate on Creative Writing from The University of Edinburgh her more practical background. She lives some-where and nowhere in Mexico, weaving new alchemy. Learn more about her at marisinthecottage.com

Also by The Authors

Not a Myth (The Faoinsgeul Woods 1)

The Fable of Wonderland

* 9 7 9 8 3 4 8 4 8 8 4 0 6 *